WINE FROM THESE GRAPES

Wine
From These Grapes

BY

EDNA ST. VINCENT MILLAY

Harper & Brothers *Publishers*
New York *and* London

"Wine from these grapes I shall be treading surely
Morning and noon and night until I die.
Stained with these grapes I shall lie down to die."
                              —*The Buck in the Snow*

CONTENTS

WINE FROM THESE GRAPES

I

II

III

IV

V

EPITAPH FOR THE RACE OF MAN

WINE FROM THESE GRAPES

I

THE RETURN

Earth does not understand her child,
  Who from the loud gregarious town
Returns, depleted and defiled,
  To the still woods, to fling him down.

Earth can not count the sons she bore:
  The wounded lynx, the wounded man
Come trailing blood unto her door;
  She shelters both as best she can.

But she is early up and out,
  To trim the year or strip its bones;
She has no time to stand about
  Talking of him in undertones

Who has no aim but to forget,
  Be left in peace, be lying thus
For days, for years, for centuries yet,
  Unshaven and anonymous;

Who, marked for failure, dulled by grief,
  Has traded in his wife and friend
For this warm ledge, this alder leaf:
  Comfort that does not comprehend.

OCTOBER—AN ETCHING

THERE where the woodcock his long bill among the
    alders
Forward in level flight propels,
Tussocks of faded grass are islands in the pasture
    swamp
Where the small foot, if it be light as well, can pass
Dry-shod to rising ground.

Not so the boot of the hunter.
Chilly and black and halfway to the knee
Is the thick water there, heavy wading,
Uneven to the step; there the more cautious ones,
Pausing for a moment, break their guns.
There the white setter ticked with black
Sets forth with silky feathers on the bird's track
And wet to his pink skin and half his size comes
    back.

Cows are pastured there; they have made a path
    among the alders.
By now the keeper's boy has found
The chalk of the woodcock on the trampled ground.

4

AUTUMN DAYBREAK

Cold wind of autumn, blowing loud
At dawn, a fortnight overdue,
Jostling the doors, and tearing through
My bedroom to rejoin the cloud,

I know—for I can hear the hiss
And scrape of leaves along the floor—
How many boughs, lashed bare by this,
Will rake the cluttered sky once more.

Tardy, and somewhat south of east,
The sun will rise at length, made known
More by the meagre light increased
Than by a disk in splendour shown;

When, having but to turn my head,
Through the stripped maple I shall see,
Bleak and remembered, patched with red,
The hill all summer hid from me.

THE OAK-LEAVES

YET in the end, defeated too, worn out and ready
   to fall,
Hangs from the drowsy tree with cramped and
   desperate stem above the ditch the last leaf
   of all.

There is something to be learned, I guess, from
   looking at the dead leaves under the living tree;
Something to be set to a lusty tune and learned and
   sung, it well might be;
Something to be learned—though I was ever a ten-
   o'clock scholar at this school—
Even perhaps by me.

But my heart goes out to the oak-leaves that are the
   last to sigh
"Enough," and loose their hold;
They have boasted to the nudging frost and to the
   two-and-thirty winds that they would never
   die,
Never even grow old.
(These are those russet leaves that cling
All winter, even into the spring,
To the dormant bough, in the wood knee-deep in
   snow the only coloured thing.)

THE FLEDGLING

So, ART thou feathered, art thou flown,
Thou naked thing?—and canst alone
Upon the unsolid summer air
Sustain thyself, and prosper there?

Shall I no more with anxious note
Advise thee through the happy day,
Thrusting the worm into thy throat,
Bearing thine excrement away?

Alas, I think I see thee yet,
Perched on the windy parapet,
Defer thy flight a moment still
To clean thy wing with careful bill.

And thou art feathered, thou art flown;
And hast a project of thine own.

THE HEDGE OF HEMLOCKS

SOMEBODY long ago
Set out this hedge of hemlocks; brought from the
woods, I'd say,
Saplings ten inches tall, curving and delicate, not
shaped like trees,
And set them out, to shut the marshes from the
lawn,
A hedge of ferns.

Four feet apart he set them, far apart, leaving
them room to grow   .   .   .
Whose crowded lower boughs these fifty years at
least
Are spiky stumps outthrust in all directions, dry,
dropping scaly bark, in the deep shade making
a thick
Dust which here and there floats in a short dazzling
beam.

Green tops, delicate and curving yet, above this
fence of brush, like ferns,
You have done well: more than the marshes now is
shut away from his protected dooryard;
The mountain, too, is shut away; not even the
wind

May trespass here to stir the purple phlox in the
   tall grass.

And yet how easily one afternoon between
Your stems, unheard, snapping no twig, dislodging
   no shell of loosened bark, unseen
Even by the spider through whose finished web he
   walked, and left it as he found it,
A neighbour entered.

CAP D'ANTIBES

THE storm is over, and the land has forgotten the
    storm; the trees are still.
Under this sun the rain dries quickly.
Cones from the sea-pines cover the ground again
Where yesterday for my fire I gathered all in sight;
But the leaves are meek. The smell of the small
    alyssum that grows wild here
Is in the air. It is a childish morning.

More sea than land am I; my sulky mind, whipped
    high by tempest in the night, is not so soon
    appeased.
Into my occupations with dull roar
It washes,
It recedes.
Even as at my side in the calm day the disturbed
    Mediterranean
Lurches with heavy swell against the bird-twittering
    shore.

FROM A TRAIN WINDOW

PRECIOUS in the light of the early sun the Housa-
   tonic
Between its not unscalable mountains flows.
Precious in the January morning the shabby fur of
   the cat-tails by the stream.
The farmer driving his horse to the feed-store for
   a sack of cracked corn
Is not in haste; there is no whip in the socket.

Pleasant enough, gay even, by no means sad
Is the rickety graveyard on the hill. Those are not
   cypress trees
Perpendicular among the lurching slabs, but cedars
   from the neighbourhood,
Native to this rocky land, self-sown. Precious
In the early light, reassuring
Is the grave-scarred hillside.
As if after all, the earth might know what it is
   about.

THE FAWN

THERE it was I saw what I shall never forget
And never retrieve.
Monstrous and beautiful to human eyes, hard to
    believe,
He lay, yet there he lay,
Asleep on the moss, his head on his polished cleft
    small ebony hooves,
The child of the doe, the dappled child of the deer.

Surely his mother had never said, "Lie here
Till I return," so spotty and plain to see
On the green moss lay he.
His eyes had opened; he considered me.

I would have given more than I care to say
To thrifty ears, might I have had him for my friend
One moment only of that forest day:

Might I have had the acceptance, not the love
Of those clear eyes;
Might I have been for him the bough above
Or the root beneath his forest bed,
A part of the forest, seen without surprise.

Was it alarm, or was it the wind of my fear lest he
    depart
That jerked him to his jointy knees,
And sent him crashing off, leaping and stumbling
On his new legs, between the stems of the white
    trees?

II

VALENTINE

Oh, what a shining town were Death
Woke you therein, and drew your breath,
My buried love; and all you were,
Caught up and cherished, even there.
Those evil windows loved of none
Would blaze as if they caught the sun.

Woke you in Heaven, Death's kinder name,
And downward in sweet gesture came
From your cold breast your rigid hand,
Then Heaven would be my native land.

But you are nowhere: you are gone
All roads into Oblivion.
Whither I would disperse, till then
From home a banished citizen.

IN THE GRAVE NO FLOWER

Here dock and tare.
But there
No flower.

Here beggar-ticks, 'tis true;
Here the rank-smelling
Thorn-apple,—and who
Would plant this by his dwelling?
Here every manner of weed
To mock the faithful harrow:
Thistles, that feed
None but the finches; yarrow,
Blue vervain, yellow charlock; here
Bindweed, that chokes the struggling year;
Broad plantain and narrow.

But there no flower.

The rye is vexed and thinned,
The wheat comes limping home,
By vetch and whiteweed harried, and the
    sandy bloom
Of the sour-grass; here
Dandelions,—and the wind
Will blow them everywhere.

18

Save there.
There
No flower.

CHILDHOOD IS THE KINGDOM WHERE NOBODY DIES

Childhood is not from birth to a certain age and
    at a certain age
The child is grown, and puts away childish things.

Childhood is the kingdom where nobody dies.

Nobody that matters, that is. Distant relatives of
    course
Die, whom one never has seen or has seen for an
    hour,
And they gave one candy in a pink-and-green
    stripèd bag, or a jack-knife,
And went away, and cannot really be said to have
    lived at all.

And cats die. They lie on the floor and lash their tails,
And their reticent fur is suddenly all in motion
With fleas that one never knew were there,
Polished and brown, knowing all there is to know,
Trekking off into the living world.
You fetch a shoe-box, but it's much too small,
    because she won't curl up now:
So you find a bigger box, and bury her in the yard,
    and weep.

But you do not wake up a month from then, two
    months,
A year from then, two years, in the middle of the
    night
And weep, with your knuckles in your mouth, and
    say Oh, God! Oh, God!

Childhood is the kingdom where nobody dies that
    matters,—mothers and fathers don't die.

And if you have said, "For heaven's sake, must you
    always be kissing a person?"
Or, "I do wish to gracious you'd stop tapping on
    the window with your thimble!"
Tomorrow, or even the day after tomorrow if you're
    busy having fun,
Is plenty of time to say, "I'm sorry, mother."

To be grown up is to sit at the table with people
    who have died, who neither listen nor speak;
Who do not drink their tea, though they always
    said
Tea was such a comfort.

Run down into the cellar and bring up the last jar
    of raspberries; they are not tempted.

Flatter them, ask them what was it they said exactly
That time, to the bishop, or to the overseer, or to Mrs. Mason;
They are not taken in.
Shout at them, get red in the face, rise,
Drag them up out of their chairs by their stiff shoulders and shake them and yell at them;
They are not startled, they are not even embarrassed; they slide back into their chairs.

Your tea is cold now.
You drink it standing up,
And leave the house.

THE SOLID SPRITE WHO STANDS ALONE

THE solid sprite who stands alone,
    And walks the world with equal stride,
Grieve though he may, is not undone
    Because a friend has died.

He knows that man is born to care,
    And ten and threescore's all his span;
And this is comfort and to spare
    For such a level man.

He is not made like crooked me,
    Who cannot rise nor lift my head,
And all because what had to be
    Has been, what lived is dead;

Who lie among my tears and rust,
    And all because a mortal brain
That loved to think, is clogged with dust,
    And will not think again.

SPRING IN THE GARDEN

Ah, CANNOT the curled shoots of the larkspur that
    you loved so,
Cannot the spiny poppy that no winter kills
Instruct you how to return through the thawing
    ground and the thin snow
Into this April sun that is driving the mist between
    the hills?

A good friend to the monkshood in a time of need
You were, and the lupine's friend as well;
But I see the lupine lift the ground like a tough weed
And the earth over the monkshood swell

And I fear that not a root in all this heaving sea
Of land, has nudged you where you lie, has found
Patience and time to direct you, numb and stupid
    as you still must be
From your first winter underground.

SONNET

Time, that renews the tissues of this frame,
That built the child and hardened the soft bone,
Taught him to wail, to blink, to walk alone,
Stare, question, wonder, give the world a name,
Forget the watery darkness whence he came,
Attends no less the boy to manhood grown,
Brings him new raiment, strips him of his own;
All skins are shed at length, remorse, even shame.

Such hope is mine, if this indeed be true,
I dread no more the first white in my hair,
Or even age itself, the easy shoe,
The cane, the wrinkled hands, the special chair:
Time, doing this to me, may alter too
My sorrow, into something I can bear.

III

AUBADE

Cool and beautiful as the blossom of the wild
    carrot
With its crimson central eye,
Round and beautiful as the globe of the onion
    blossom
Were her pale breasts whereon I laid me down to die.

From the wound of my enemy that thrust me
    through in the dark wood
I arose; with sweat on my lip and the wild wood-
    grasses in my spur
I arose and stood.
But never did I arise from loving her.

SAPPHO CROSSES THE DARK RIVER
INTO HADES

Charon, indeed, your dreaded oar,
With what a peaceful sound it dips
Into the stream; how gently, too,
From the wet blade the water drips.

I knew a ferryman before.
But he was not so old as you.
He spoke from unembittered lips,
With careless eyes on the bright sea
One day, such bitter words to me
As age and wisdom never knew.

This was a man of meagre fame;
He ferried merchants from the shore
To Mitylene (whence I came)
On Lesbos; Phaon is his name.

I hope that he will never die,
As I have done, and come to dwell
In this pale city we approach.
Not that, indeed, I wish him well,
(Though never have I wished him harm)
But rather that I hope to find
In some unechoing street of Hell
The peace I long have had in mind:

A peace whereon may not encroach
That supple back, the strong brown arm,
That curving mouth, the sunburned curls;
But rather that I would rely,
Having come so far, at such expense,
Upon some quiet lodging whence
I need not hear his voice go by
In scraps of talk with boys and girls.

IV

EPITAPH

GRIEVE not for happy Claudius, he is dead;
And empty is his skull.
Pity no longer, arm-in-arm with Dread,
Walks in that polished hall.

Joy, too, is fled.
But no man can have all.

ON THOUGHT IN HARNESS

MY FALCON to my wrist
Returns
From no high air.
I sent her toward the sun that burns ·
Above the mist;
But she has not been there.

Her talons are not cold; her beak
Is closed upon no wonder;
Her head stinks of its hood, her feathers reek
Of me, that quake at the thunder.

Degraded bird, I give you back your eyes for-
      ever, ascend now whither you are tossed;
Forsake this wrist, forsake this rhyme;
Soar, eat ether, see what has never been seen;
      depart, be lost,
But climb.

DESOLATION DREAMED OF

DESOLATION dreamed of, though not accomplished,
Set my heart to rocking like a boat in a swell.
To every face I met, I said farewell.

Green rollers breaking white along a clean beach . . .
*   when shall I reach that island?*
Gladly, O painted nails and shaven arm-pits, would
*   I see less of you!*
Gladly, gladly would I be far from you for a long time,
*   O noise and stench of man!*

I said farewell. Nevertheless,
Whom have I quitted?—which of my possessions
    do I propose to leave?
Not one. This feigning to be asleep when wide
    awake is all the loneliness
I shall ever achieve.

THE LEAF AND THE TREE

When will you learn, my self, to be
A dying leaf on a living tree?
Budding, swelling, growing strong,
Wearing green, but not for long,
Drawing sustenance from air,
That other leaves, and you not there,
May bud, and at the autumn's call
Wearing russet, ready to fall?

Has not this trunk a deed to do
Unguessed by small and tremulous you?
Shall not these branches in the end
To wisdom and the truth ascend?
And the great lightning plunging by
Look sidewise with a golden eye
To glimpse a tree so tall and proud
It sheds its leaves upon a cloud?

Here, I think, is the heart's grief:
The tree, no mightier than the leaf,
Makes firm its root and spreads its crown
And stands; but in the end comes down.
That airy top no boy could climb
Is trodden in a little time
By cattle on their way to drink.
The fluttering thoughts a leaf can think,

That hears the wind and waits its turn,
Have taught it all a tree can learn.

Time can make soft that iron wood.
The tallest trunk that ever stood,
In time, without a dream to keep,
Crawls in beside the root to sleep.

ON THE WIDE HEATH

On the wide heath at evening overtaken,
 When the fast-reddening sun
Drops, and against the sky the looming bracken
 Waves, and the day is done,

Though no unfriendly nostril snuffs his bone,
 Though English wolves be dead,
The fox abroad on errands of his own,
 The adder gone to bed,

The weary traveler from his aching hip
 Lengthens his long stride;
Though Home be but a humming on his lip,
 No happiness, no pride,

He does not drop him under the yellow whin
 To sleep the darkness through;
Home to the yellow light that shines within
 The kitchen of a loud shrew,

Home over stones and sand, through stagnant
 water
 He goes, mile after mile
Home to a wordless poaching son and a daughter
 With a disdainful smile,

Home to the worn reproach, the disagreeing,
  The shelter, the stale air; content to be
Pecked at, confined, encroached upon,—it being
  Too lonely, to be free.

APOSTROPHE TO MAN

(on reflecting that the world is ready to go to war again)

DETESTABLE race, continue to expunge yourself,
    die out.
Breed faster, crowd, encroach, sing hymns, build
    bombing air-planes;
Make speeches, unveil statues, issue bonds, parade;
Convert again into explosives the bewildered am-
    monia and the distracted cellulose;
Convert again into putrescent matter drawing flies
The hopeful bodies of the young; exhort,
Pray, pull long faces, be earnest, be all but over-
    come, be photographed;
Confer, perfect your formulae, commercialize
Bacteria harmful to human tissue,
Put death on the market;
Breed, crowd, encroach, expand, expunge yourself,
    die out,
Homo called *sapiens*.

TWO SONNETS IN MEMORY

(Nicola Sacco—Bartolomeo Vanzetti)
Executed August 23, 1927

I

As men have loved their lovers in times past
And sung their wit, their virtue and their grace,
So have we loved sweet Justice to the last,
That now lies here in an unseemly place.
The child will quit the cradle and grow wise
And stare on beauty till his senses drown;
Yet shall be seen no more by mortal eyes
Such beauty as here walked and here went down.
Like birds that hear the winter crying plain
Her courtiers leave to seek the clement south;
Many have praised her, we alone remain
To break a fist against the lying mouth
Of any man who says this was not so:
Though she be dead now, as indeed we know.

II

Where can the heart be hidden in the ground
And be at peace, and be at peace forever,
Under the world, untroubled by the sound
Of mortal tears, that cease from pouring never?
Well for the heart, by stern compassion harried,
If death be deeper than the churchmen say,—
Gone from this world indeed what's graveward
    carried,
And laid to rest indeed what's laid away.
Anguish enough while yet the indignant breather
Have blood to spurt upon the oppressor's hand;
Who would eternal be, and hang in ether
A stuffless ghost above his struggling land,
Retching in vain to render up the groan
That is not there, being aching dust's alone?

MY SPIRIT, SORE FROM MARCHING

My spirit, sore from marching
   Toward that receding west
Where Pity shall be governor,
   With Wisdom for his guest:

Lie down beside these waters
   That bubble from the spring;
Hear in the desert silence
   The desert sparrow sing;

Draw from the shapeless moment
   Such pattern as you can;
And cleave henceforth to Beauty;
   Expect no more from man.

Man, with his ready answer,
   His sad and hearty word,
For every cause in limbo,
   For every debt deferred,

For every pledge forgotten,
   His eloquent and grim
Deep empty gaze upon you,—
   Expect no more from him.

From cool and aimless Beauty
　　Your bread and comfort take,
Beauty, that made no promise,
　　And has no word to break;

Have eyes for Beauty only,
　　That has no eyes for you;
Follow her struck pavilion,
　　Halt with her retinue;

Catch from the board of Beauty
　　Such careless crumbs as fall.
Here's hope for priest and layman;
　　Here's heresy for all.

CONSCIENTIOUS OBJECTOR

I SHALL die, but that is all that I shall do for
    Death.

I hear him leading his horse out of the stall; I hear
    the clatter on the barn-floor.
He is in haste; he has business in Cuba, business in
    the Balkans, many calls to make this morning.
But I will not hold the bridle while he cinches the
    girth.
And he may mount by himself: I will not give him a
    leg up.

Though he flick my shoulders with his whip, I will
    not tell him which way the fox ran.
With his hoof on my breast, I will not tell him where
    the black boy hides in the swamp.
I shall die, but that is all that I shall do for Death;
    I am not on his pay-roll.

I will not tell him the whereabouts of my friends
    nor of my enemies either.
Though he promise me much, I will not map him
    the route to any man's door.

Am I a spy in the land of the living, that I should
deliver men to Death?
Brother, the password and the plans of our city are
safe with me; never through me
Shall you be overcome.

ABOVE THESE CARES

ABOVE these cares my spirit in calm abiding
Floats like a swimmer at sunrise, facing the pale sky;
Peaceful, heaved by the light infrequent lurch of
the heavy wave serenely sliding
Under his weightless body, aware of the wide morn-
ing, aware of the gull on the red buoy bedaubed
with guano, aware of his sharp cry;
Idly athirst for the sea, as who should say:
In a moment I will roll upon my mouth and drink
it dry.

Painfully, under the pressure that obtains
At the sea's bottom, crushing my lungs and my
brains
(For the body makes shift to breathe and after a
fashion flourish
Ten fathoms deep in care,
Ten fathoms down in an element denser than air
Wherein the soul must perish)
I trap and harvest, stilling my stomach's needs;
I crawl forever, hoping never to see
Above my head the limbs of my spirit no longer free
Kicking in frenzy, a swimmer enmeshed in weeds.

IF STILL YOUR ORCHARDS BEAR

BROTHER, that breathe the August air
  Ten thousand years from now,
And smell—if still your orchards bear
  Tart apples on the bough—

The early windfall under the tree,
  And see the red fruit shine,
I cannot think your thoughts will be
  Much different from mine.

Should at that moment the full moon
  Step forth upon the hill,
And memories hard to bear at noon,
  By moonlight harder still,

Form in the shadows of the trees,—
  Things that you could not spare
And live, or so you thought, yet these
  All gone, and you still there,

A man no longer what he was,
  Nor yet the thing he'd planned,
The chilly apple from the grass
  Warmed by your living hand—

I think you will have need of tears;
I think they will not flow;
Supposing in ten thousand years
Men ache, as they do now.

LINES FOR A GRAVE-STONE

Man alive, that mournst thy lot,
Desiring what thou hast not got,
Money, beauty, love, what not,

Deeming it blesseder to be
A rotted man than live to see
So rude a sky as covers thee,

Deeming thyself of all unblest
And wretched souls the wretchedest,
Longing to die and be at rest:

Know that however grim the fate
That sent thee forth to meditate
Upon my enviable state,

Here lieth one that would resign
Gladly his lot, to shoulder thine.
Give me thy coat; get into mine.

HOW NAKED, HOW WITHOUT A WALL

How naked, how without a wall
  Against the wind and the sharp sleet,
He fares at night, that fares at all
  Forth from the stove's heat.

Or if the moon be in the sky,
  Or if the stars, and the late moon
Not rising till an hour goes by,
  And Libra setting soon,

How naked, how without a stitch
  To shut him from the earnest air,
He goes, that by the whispering ditch
  Alone at night will fare.

Nor is it but the rising chill
  From the warm weeds, that strikes him cold;
Nor that the stridulant hedge grows still,
  Like what has breath to hold,

Until his tiny foot go past
  At length, with its enormous sound;
Nor yet his helpless shadow cast
  To any wolf around.

Bare to the moon and her cold rays
    He takes the road, who by and by
Goes bare beneath the moony gaze
    Of his own awful eye.

He sees his motive, like a fox
    Hid in a badger's hole; he sees
His honour, strangled, in a box,
    Her neck lashed to her knees.

The man who ventures forth alone
    When other men are snug within
Walks on his marrow, not his bone,
    And lacks his outer skin.

The draughty caverns of his breath
    Grow visible, his heart shines through:
Surely a thing which only death
    Can have the right to do.

V

EPITAPH FOR THE RACE OF MAN

I

Before this cooling planet shall be cold,
Long, long before the music of the Lyre,
Like the faint roar of distant breakers rolled
On reefs unseen, when wind and flood conspire
To drive the ship inshore—long, long, I say,
Before this ominous humming hits the ear,
Earth will have come upon a stiller day,
Man and his engines be no longer here.
High on his naked rock the mountain sheep
Will stand alone against the final sky,
Drinking a wind of danger new and deep,
Staring on Vega with a piercing eye,
And gather up his slender hooves and leap
From crag to crag down Chaos, and so go by.

II

WHEN Death was young and bleaching bones
  were few,
A moving hill against the risen day
The dinosaur at morning made his way,
And dropped his dung upon the blazing dew;
Trees with no name that now are agate grew
Lushly beside him in the steamy clay;
He woke and hungered, rose and stalked his
  prey,
And slept contented, in a world he knew.
In punctual season, with the race in mind,
His consort held aside her heavy tail,
And took the seed; and heard the seed confined
Roar in her womb; and made a nest to hold
A hatched-out conqueror . . . but to
  no avail:
The veined and fertile eggs are long since cold.

III

CRETACEOUS bird, your giant claw no lime
From bark of holly bruised or mistletoe
Could have arrested, could have held you so
Through fifty million years of jostling time;
Yet cradled with you in the catholic slime
Of the young ocean's tepid lapse and flow
Slumbered an agent, weak in embryo,
Should grip you straitly, in its sinewy prime.
What bright collision in the zodiac brews,
What mischief dimples at the planet's core
For shark, for python, for the dove that coos
Under the leaves?—what frosty fate's in store
For the warm blood of man,—man, out of ooze
But lately crawled, and climbing up the shore?

IV

O EARTH, unhappy planet born to die,
Might I your scribe and your confessor be,
What wonders must you not relate to me
Of Man, who when his destiny was high
Strode like the sun into the middle sky
And shone an hour, and who so bright as he,
And like the sun went down into the sea,
Leaving no spark to be remembered by.
But no; you have not learned in all these years
To tell the leopard and the newt apart;
Man, with his singular laughter, his droll tears,
His engines and his conscience and his art,
Made but a simple sound upon your ears:
The patient beating of the animal heart.

V

WHEN Man is gone and only gods remain
To stride the world, their mighty bodies hung
With golden shields, and golden curls outflung
Above their childish foreheads; when the plain
Round skull of Man is lifted and again
Abandoned by the ebbing wave, among
The sand and pebbles of the beach,—what tongue
Will tell the marvel of the human brain?
Heavy with music once this windy shell,
Heavy with knowledge of the clustered stars;
The one-time tenant of this draughty hall
Himself, in learned pamphlet, did foretell,
After some aeons of study jarred by wars,
This toothy gourd, this head emptied of all.

VI

See where Capella with her golden kids
Grazes the slope between the east and north?
Thus when the builders of the pyramids
Flung down their tools at nightfall and poured forth
Homeward to supper and a poor man's bed,
Shortening the road with friendly jest and slur,
The risen She-Goat showing blue and red
Climbed the clear dusk, and three stars followed her.
Safe in their linen and their spices lie
The kings of Egypt; even as long ago
Under these constellations, with long eye
And scented limbs they slept, and feared no foe.
Their will was law; their will was not to die:
And so they had their way; or nearly so.

VII

He heard the coughing tiger in the night
Push at his door; close by his quiet head
About the wattled cabin the soft tread
Of heavy feet he followed, and the slight
Sigh of the long banana leaves; in sight
At last and leaning westward overhead
The Centaur and the Cross now heralded
The sun, far off but marching, bringing light.
What time the Centaur and the Cross were spent
Night and the beast retired into the hill,
Whereat serene and undevoured he lay,
And dozed and stretched and listened and lay still,
Breathing into his body with content
The temperate dawn before the tropic day.

VIII

Observe how Miyanoshita cracked in two
And slid into the valley; he that stood
Grinning with terror in the bamboo wood
Saw the earth heave and thrust its bowels through
The hill, and his own kitchen slide from view,
Spilling the warm bowl of his humble food
Into the lap of horror; mark how lewd
This cluttered gulf,—'twas here his paddy grew.
Dread and dismay have not encompassed him;
The calm sun sets; unhurried and aloof
Into the riven village falls the rain;
Days pass; the ashes cool; he builds again
His paper house upon oblivion's brim,
And plants the purple iris in its roof.

IX

HE WOKE in terror to a sky more bright
Than middle day; he heard the sick earth groan,
And ran to see the lazy-smoking cone
Of the fire-mountain, friendly to his sight
As his wife's hand, gone strange and full of fright;
Over his fleeing shoulder it was shown
Rolling its pitchy lake of scalding stone
Upon his house that had no feet for flight.
Where did he weep? Where did he sit him down
And sorrow, with his head between his knees?
Where said the Race of Man, "Here let me drown"?
"Here let me die of hunger"?—"let me freeze"?
By nightfall he has built another town:
This boiling pot, this clearing in the trees.

X

THE broken dike, the levee washed away,
The good fields flooded and the cattle drowned,
Estranged and treacherous all the faithful ground,
And nothing left but floating disarray
Of tree and home uprooted,—was this the day
Man dropped upon his shadow without a sound
And died, having laboured well and having found
His burden heavier than a quilt of clay?
No, no. I saw him when the sun had set
In water, leaning on his single oar
Above his garden faintly glimmering yet . . .
There bulked the plough, here washed the updrifted
    weeds . . .
And scull across his roof and make for shore,
With twisted face and pocket full of seeds.

XI

Sweeter was loss than silver coins to spend,
Sweeter was famine than the belly filled;
Better than blood in the vein was the blood spilled;
Better than corn and healthy flocks to tend
And a tight roof and acres without end
Was the barn burned and the mild creatures killed,
And the back aging fast, and all to build:
For then it was, his neighbour was his friend.
Then for a moment the averted eye
Was turned upon him with benignant beam,
Defiance faltered, and derision slept;
He saw as in a not unhappy dream
The kindly heads against the horrid sky,
And scowled, and cleared his throat and spat, and
    wept.

XII

Now forth to meadow as the farmer goes
With shining buckets to the milking-ground,
He meets the black ant hurrying from his mound
To milk the aphis pastured on the rose;
But no good-morrow, as you might suppose,
No nod of greeting, no perfunctory sound
Passes between them; no occasion's found
For gossip as to how the fodder grows.
In chilly autumn on the hardening road
They meet again, driving their flocks to stall,
Two herdsmen, each with winter for a goad;
They meet and pass, and never a word at all
Gives one to t'other. On the quaint abode
Of each, the evening and the first snow fall.

XIII

His heatless room the watcher of the stars
Nightly inhabits when the night is clear;
Propping his mattress on the turning sphere,
Saturn his rings or Jupiter his bars
He follows, or the fleeing moons of Mars,
Till from his ticking lens they disappear. . . .
Whereat he sighs, and yawns, and on his ear
The busy chirp of Earth remotely jars.
Peace at the void's heart through the wordless night,
A lamb cropping the awful grasses, grazed;
Earthward the trouble lies, where strikes his light
At dawn industrious Man, and unamazed
Goes forth to plough, flinging a ribald stone
At all endeavour alien to his own.

XIV

Him not the golden fang of furious heaven,
Nor whirling Aeolus on his awful wheel,
Nor foggy specter ramming the swift keel,
Nor flood, nor earthquake, nor the red tongue even
Of fire, disaster's dog—him, him bereaven
Of all save the heart's knocking, and to feel
The air upon his face: not the great heel
Of headless Force into the dust has driven.
These sunken cities, tier on tier, bespeak
How ever from the ashes with proud beak
And shining feathers did the phoenix rise,
And sail, and send the vulture from the skies . . .
That in the end returned; for Man was weak
Before the unkindness in his brother's eyes.

XV

Now sets his foot upon the eastern sill
Aldebaran, swiftly rising, mounting high,
And tracks the Pleiads down the crowded sky,
And drives his wedge into the western hill;
Now for the void sets forth, and further still,
The questioning mind of Man . . . that by and by
From the void's rim returns with swooning eye,
Having seen himself into the maelstrom spill.
Blench not, O race of Adam, lest you find
In the sun's bubbling bowl anonymous death,
Or lost in whistling space without a mind
To monstrous Nothing yield your little breath:
You shall achieve destruction where you stand,
In intimate conflict, at your brother's hand.

XVI

ALAS for Man, so stealthily betrayed,
Bearing the bad cell in him from the start,
Pumping and feeding from his healthy heart
That wild disorder never to be stayed
When once established, destined to invade
With angry hordes the true and proper part,
Till Reason joggles in the headsman's cart,
And Mania spits from every balustrade.
Would he had searched his closet for his bane,
Where lurked the trusted ancient of his soul,
Obsequious Greed, and seen that visage plain;
Would he had whittled treason from his side
In his stout youth and bled his body whole,
Then had he died a king, or never died.

XVII

Only the diamond and the diamond's dust
Can render up the diamond unto Man;
One and invulnerable as it began
Had it endured, but for the treacherous thrust
That laid its hard heart open, as it must,
And ground it down and fitted it to span
A turbaned brow or fret an ivory fan,
Lopped of its stature, pared of its proper crust.
So Man, by all the wheels of heaven unscored,
Man, the stout ego, the exuberant mind,
No edge could cleave, no acid could consume,
Being split along the vein by his own kind,
Gives over, rolls upon the palm abhorred,
Is set in brass on the swart thumb of Doom.

XVIII

Here lies, and none to mourn him but the sea,
That falls incessant on the empty shore,
Most various Man, cut down to spring no more;
Before his prime, even in his infancy
Cut down, and all the clamour that was he,
Silenced; and all the riveted pride he wore,
A rusted iron column whose tall core
The rains have tunnelled like an aspen tree.
Man, doughty Man, what power has brought you
    low,
That heaven itself in arms could not persuade
To lay aside the lever and the spade
And be as dust among the dusts that blow?
Whence, whence the broadside? whose the heavy
    blade? . . .
Strive not to speak, poor scattered mouth; I know.